Mother, Can I Say It Now?

David Groulx

Copyright © 2025 by David Groulx

All rights reserved. No part of this publication may be reproduced or transmitted in any form or by any means, electronic or mechanical, including photocopying, recording or any information storage and retrieval, without the written permission of the publisher. Names, characters, places and incidents are either the product of the author's imagination or used fictitiously, and any resemblance to actual persons living or dead, events or locales is entirely coincidental. All trademarks are properties of their respective owners.

Published by
BookLand Press Inc.
15 Allstate Parkway, Suite 600
Markham, Ontario L3R 5B4
www.booklandpress.com

Printed in Canada

Front cover image by Garry Killian

Library and Archives Canada Cataloguing in Publication

Title: Mother, can I say it now? / David Groulx.
Names: Groulx, David, 1969- author.
Series: Modern Indigenous voices.
Description: Series statement: Modern Indigenous voices
Identifiers: Canadiana (print) 20250122952 | Canadiana (ebook) 20250122979 | ISBN 9781772312447 (softcover) | ISBN 9781772312454 (EPUB)
Subjects: LCGFT: Poetry.
Classification: LCC PS8563.R76 C36 2025 | DDC C811/.54—dc23

We acknowledge the support of the Government of Canada through the Canada Book Fund. We acknowledge the support of the Canada Council for the Arts. We acknowledge funding support from the Ontario Arts Council and the Government of Ontario.

Mother, Can I Say It Now?

Table of Contents

A word that means belonging to the morning | 7

My street is not a word for tragedy | 8

Pow | 11

To be sung while 'washing of the dead' | 12

Climate (de) range | 15

Cata-strophe hammering | 16

Musica-ficta | 20

This poem is a safe space | 23

Aphasia: sun driven from our faces | 24

Letter 01 | 29

Letter 02 | 31

Letter 03 | 32

My 11th Billy the Kid poem | 33

The next pretend-Indian | 34

Stranger: manic | 36

What to wish for | 38

And one who gathers | 39

I hate my father's Sunday poems | 40

SYSM is a shut your savage mouth system TIC | 41

Pandemics making-me-manic | 43

Antiphon with a digging sound | 44

Maid in Hollywood | 45

While I cut peaches and the phone rings | 46

Finding white space | 48

Remember Nancy | 49

Porsches not people poem | 50

Song in the manner of the military | 51

Sheets to die for | 52

This is way I am kind to strangers | 53

Food issues | 54

Plant food | 55

Voting me off the island | 56

Transference | 57

A cemetery in Gaza | 58

Speaking to the average Joe with inner voice | 59

Things abandon in the night | 61

Eden beside the highway | 62

I ain't that cat-in-the-box and nether are you | 64

Stromata | 65

A word that means belonging to the morning

My ear moves to thy voice like zephyrs,
over the green grasses of summer

The Whiteman's burden is his creation
and my burden.

God destroys that,
which was born unlucky.

starvation is always trending
the only green left on earth will be gangrene

If I were wise I'd cut out my tongue and
stance more chance to be love(d).

Your existence is a trope

or be a bird moving over continents
move continuants
wish to be a bird

a sad trope.

thus saith Sartre.

My street is not a word for tragedy

The sirens did not die here, in a Greek tragedy
they moved here
to my street.

they came here like being pulled up flowers, then
falling with force.

Citizens said they came because they wanted our jobs
I found that hard to believe
leave home to come here to.

flip-clean toilets-drive to a better life,
somewhere else.

      On my street the rules were simple,
        because *it lives* like this,

On my street, there's a woman who walks
four times around of her home before sunrise,
this is the way she orders the world.

She remembers something tragic.
On my street are people
who've made choices I've never had to make.

On my street, tenements' burn down
and condos are built there place,
it begins to move two dimensional.

On my street, people carry pieces of God
nobody else wanted.
On my street my friend lost his girl to an overdose,

he found her dead on the couch.
My life becomes a grave for your entire heart.
Everyone is an allegory for something.
We walked to the bus-stop to work together that morning,
it was like he wanted to hold my hand. *but*

On my street shit like that ain't allowed.
On my street there is a woman dying of loneliness,
but has to take care of her mother first.

On my street the convenience store,
products are marked,
"Not for resale in Canada."

On my street, a young boy stabbed
his grandmother to death,
but because addiction is seen a failure of the individual,
instead of society.

On my street there is an ice cream truck that sells cocaine
instead of ice cream because life is cheaper, and
its all one flavour anyways.

On my street a man was shot to death, by a teenager
stoned in his head, cameras came asking
people to shit on their neighbours,
I just kinda stared at them till they left.

they did not care about anything else.
On my street, houses are mailboxes with tombs attached.

On My street God has murdered all hope,
of ever having any,
and the Lord had mercy, but we needed money.
for the other lord

On my street, there's a woman
who grows tiny red tomatoes
and in the fall, I eat them in exchange
for poems that are suicidal.

On my street there's a woman who loves red wine more
than it loves her, it's not the greatest relationship,
but she depends on it.
On my street, the cops on my street
don't live on my street.
On my street, the emptiness moves.

Time is always ticking here, people hurry,
never getting home early. *they never get or go anywhere.*

My street has a big appetite,
it gets eaten by real estate agents,
developers and anyone else who doesn't live here.

The name of my street is not the name of a tragedy,
it's a word for misery.
This is the of the poor.
The disadvantaged and the shit out of luck.

Pow

When a man is abused

he goes willingly.

All the other men will gather

to see what kind of beating he can give

what kind can he take.

A fist is always a measure of character.

A cut sometimes looks like a scratch,
and a strike was struck!

Here, lions would walk away from each other
as would horses,

mooses and asses. Anything with a brain, no wait,
even jellyfish.

Here, his punch will tell you

if you will lead him or leave him.

A punch is a point and *here it is:*

You will know what you can take from this man,

and what you can give.

To be sung while 'washing of the dead'

day of wrath

Sunday morning

civilizations dull Cartesian beatitudes
of

the coffee bean came from poverty-stricken, *you name it*
    milk from a bovine destined for slaw
no sugar

life is - sweet enough.

I know a song that has no beats, no rhythms
and no sounds

haunting echoes of the universal
    emptiness

all my strophes and all my chorus
    unstood

tenor, symbol, metaphor

when it's structural, it's all you can do

to taste the acid   the song goes roar

I am iambic pentameter
you
who always bring back because you don't have
enough money to live in Montreal
or the moon.

I am the only thing right with the world
I am a natural desire
natural man-flesh
I vibrate to the low frequencies
touch the high ones
I am the pure DNA feeling flesh god

I am an ox spark
turning.

When I was young
my life was Epicures'
now I am old
Diogenes has taken hold

I need something that rhymes with the sound of a siren
to de-cauterize my neighbourhood
life is desperate
life has a grudge against us
and death loves us too much

Finding meaning is not impossible,
it's just nobody bothers with it.
we ghost the world.

The rich are slaves to
the bodies that serve them.
I went to the sun once, I never healed properly

I've found there's good bull-shitters in bars
as well as behind them

but always better ones behind pulpits and TV cameras.

You are the same now as you were as a child
only more damaged.

Whatever makes you more human,
do that.

In the last year, there was nothing and
God came to me, fashioned from nowhere,
knowing the future was death

There would be more cynics in the cities,
but all the good spots got taken up by the homeless,
but now public sex is just for shame.

w. of God

Climate (de) range

Munitions become mutations
zygotes become bygones
bye bye baby

If I am not god's idea of a man then what am I?

*I am a maker too and the light that is in me
came from you.
The universe will affirm in the event of my death.
Image(in) mind
never
where else to be
like me*

I no longer believe in beliefs
I no longer cause in causes
outside the mall is an ossuary
an inside fear of rejection-
*if you make them ashamed of themselves
they will come back.*

Cata-strophe hammering

In evening I forget hunger
I forget, am not old

and there are many
who should be here with me
and are not,

life is hard.

When poets are pushed into
poverty,
the poor are given a voice.

I come as water to the earth

sometimes as rivers sometimes as streams
sometimes as lakes sometimes as waves

raindrops, ponds, or oceans
seas, or drizzle

I fall back to earth as water,
always water.

Speech is very expensive, people who talk a lot
have a lot,

of nothing to say.

I sit with Mao every morning watching sunrise,
the tyranny of the proletariat must be supreme

(red) Thought Mao Thought
We all thought Mao,

and everyone must die of loneliness at least once.

Remember, he says, nothing gets carried into
Oz in a red river ox cart.

Humans are too emotional to be anything else
remember who you are and die that way.

w. of Mao
Let not, the flesh grieve the
spirit of God that is in you
that made you want to know of,
if not understand love.

w. of God

My wine painted red skin
I am always on the wrong side of it.

He who called me into existence, will
call me out of it.

He is the one who does not answer
because He does not hear you
He is the one, the ages know
briefly.

[I am another word-bitch for the lord.

Soon the study of dendrology
will be a branch of archaeology
w. of God

The cords of my brain stretch,
Give greatly to God, because war is for all of us
and in all of us.

I was given a god-hand
I am part of the cloth of man,

there is no definition of life only
divination and devotion.

the popped veins on my legs are like lightening strikes
mapping the places I've been.

rivers like snowflakes in shapes and patterns
my mind misses the breaks
and begins to break.
I am a Mandelbrot set of failure.]

death brings man to truths,
that God couldn't drag him to.

The answer is always, die trying.

The spirit of the lord turns again
like a belly-down horse and says,

get on you knees and write this,

Oh you,
of the God of
the sufferer of the murder of men
slaughterer of the flesh of men.

Man had lost the power of speech long ago
after the eruption of the
Lake Toba.
Now, work for an animal as animal
as a man for a man as a slave

I am the last time you will hear the voice of God
I am the last empire built in red clay
at last I am last

w. of God

Musica-ficta

My solus somewhither and withers Ra!

rain maker rain maker rain maker ha!

Hang up the harp oh great herald of the ghost of this age,

all we can find are your nails.

Poverty is misery convicting millions
open-air-prison-earth... *and biggest crime.*

The sons of serious dendrology

hung their theology on a christmas tree

Pessoa and Pound

and the moleculi of sylla-bells,

separation creation.

As a child I almost drowned in river

then I drowned my liver

because I was reliving

the wet hours of my past.

Who is of the wind pipe and of the strophe?
one arm, one leg, one loaf.

I am a toothy musky,

of a thousand fisherman's casts

on a thousand summer days,

what I touch, God palliates.

I went to the moon once,

I never healed properly.

My cat is a prayer and dreamers,

are liars who deluge years.

Everyone is welcome to live, one way

or another. I had

traumas, I didn't know I had.

So I sat with them,

and listened to the rhapsody rising

inside of me like a missing God,
and in the last year there was nothing

God came to me festooned w. blood garland,
knowing the future was death.
We hoped,

it was like a popping in the brain,
a machine snaps and breaks, finding

itself in silence.

There is NO SHAME in desire.

Men will collect me like ants on the ground

I am falling

now sky now   ants now

day of wrath.

This poem is a safe space

This poem is a safe space
This poem is a safe space
This poem is a safe space
This poem is a safe space
This poem is a safe space
This poem is a safe space
This poem is a safe space
This poem is a safe space

all are welcome all are safe here

The past only has meaning because it is done

I am not an ink you would write the would *justice* with
nor would I be the colour of a piece of paper with
the word *Indian* on it.

This poem is a safe space X8

all are welcome all are safe here

the world would hear me once
listen once
for once

I am human.

Aphasia: sun driven from our faces

I never had the ability to be loved,

or disappointed

I disappeared into the movies,

the 1st movie I disappeared into was

Black Raven, a 1943 classic noir,

mostly it was about rain.

    [disembodied voice]:
        "I think I am dying, which is just as well,
because I don't think anyone here will miss me
as I am dying and to remember anyone
here will be impossible by the time I'm through with it."

black & white

bare

like any good sickness, it progresses rapidly

like fire it consumes, it curses

and whenever I laugh it turns to tears.

The 2nd movie

I turned into was

Horror Hotel, it was like the first

but with fog, witches, and my

first wife, she was the inn keeper's widow

she was very cruel and beautiful,
but I had been blind since birth

and mistook kisses for kindness and

apologies as meaningful.

I went back to the coven
"Eye of newt, drops of snake venom
and thin haired man's lips,

a curse upon the palette."

Is it possible not to give a shit

at all?

"Bubble, bubble cauldron trouble?" am I

ever to stop telling myself,

I am an unworthy victim...

to ever feel love?

touch? My mind wants to know.

Or is that the work of the Necromancer?

Job Posting

Necromancer wanted

Evenings & weekends only
Must have own transportation
Prophets need not apply: already know truth.

Reply: Dear Sir: I am inquiring about of position of Necromancer. No. I am not a

Prophet. My acquaintance with the dead... the departed began when I was 4, you see 1

summer there was a young man in my village, mmm not village, but more of some shacks

along the highway. The young man bought himself a Plymouth Road Runner, muscle car

with the money he'd made at the mines; the car ended up killing him not long after. It was

then I began to understand forever never ends and if it does, it can only do so suffering.

[disembodied voice]:

"And now I can feel the world change when someone dies."
Like so many waves
                breaking
My dog Sam also brought me to the distances of forever when he was hit by a car later that summer, the cops stopped, finished him off right there with
a bullet from his hand gun.

I never saw

my dog again and

despised cops ever since.

I would also like to mention torch carrying and cross bearing abilities,

as I carried both for a girl named Xiomara for nine years, until I finally spoke to her and

figured

she wasn't my type.

Also I have my own flashlight batt. not incl.

[disembodied voice]:

I was beautiful once
and then the government said
I was wasn't

then everyone

said, I wasn't
half of me suffered
half of me felt nothing
and I existed this way
building symbols w/ wds recognized only by
other wds.

Letter 01

And I was dreamed into

35mm from MOMA and held like a prisoner

in the era where madness hid loneliness.

When I took it's mask off

I did not stare at it

nor look away

I did not dance with it, any longer

or ask it to dance

I did not hate it, I did not love it

Instead I wrote hymns to the cerebrospinal fluid
leaking out of my ear

My brain half submerged,
it became impossible to
register my screams into anything
a human might understand as suffering,
the other half of my brain busy, creating a new

fear of drowning.

And whatever you thought about

forever at that moment

and whatever forever is now

and now and now and now

time grows into forgetting.

My lungs painted rusted iron

and my suicide is the lord destroying his own work.

Letter 02

I am a sinner who can find no redemption is Jerusalem,
new or old

I search through your Hemlock words for the real
meaning of death,

all masks are buried in the cemeteries of your mind,
stacked

sometimes three and four high

like shadows

even ashes take up room

Who were you then? smoking in the stairwell
with other boys

that felt like accidents, never meaning to be.

If I'd been born in Tibet,
my hymns would have been punches to the sky

and open hands to the earth, and every year

I am not born in Tibet, I die somewhere else.

always building walls out of tears.

Letter 03

I will make you a songbird minced meat pie

because the dead can no longer sing

and the living trade in old traumas

for new ones.

I cannot move the oceans with my fingers,
madness never becomes mundane.

Some men only understand Auschwitz in numbers.

A body lays in a pasture forever lit by dawn,

while God too, digs the grave.

I know Dionysus said the end of pleasure
is a job you can apply for,
but nobody in the

place had the balls, so he looked at me and said

[disembodied voice]:
"I guess it'll be you and that's how I got the job

and all society ever thought of it

could fit into a circus canon to be fired by fools who thought

elephants only worked for peanuts
and disembodied voices were really their own."

My 11th Billy the Kid poem

If I could only write poems to Billy the Kid

I'd make them taste sweet like brandy & leather on the tongue

with a pen like the one that stroked Jesus' death warrant or

my own, ungifted

condemned to a toke in one hand,

the other,

completely empty

and open.

The next pretend-Indian

I want to steal back from you, everything that is me.

My fists you did not fight.

The nights I cried alone

you did not call me or hold me.

Told me you were tough, been where I been!

hustled what I hustled,

turns out no one remembered you

you weren't there

like I wanted you to be,

for me, a safe place

whenever the cops drove by me.

Now that's gone, because it

Turns out you weren't drinking tuff-stuff

with me, after all,

to kill what I was told to kill ~~in~~ myself.
Turns out you were suffering

some other kind of sadness,

but you knew that.

Turns out we weren't making love,

you and I

but one of us was getting fucked

and it wasn't you.

Stranger: manic

I've always been meaning to write this letter to you
to me
to I
to us
to you that is us and us
that is only us when I look into the mirror
and say Who is that?

I've been meaning to write this letter to you
that is me
and whoever I used to be

Sometimes it's like my head or my heart or both are
going to explode

and anyway, I don't know how you made it here
and good luck with the rest of it
I suppose nobody knows how it ends anyway.

I've been meaning to speak to you
to I
to us
to me that is we
and whoever we used to be
whenever I look in the mirror

I wanted to say it took a lot of me to get you here,
the health
the wealth
the worry and warts
It was me
me that is we
and you that is me
and me that is you
that got you through and we'll see you at or near the end

where you'll say to me
it was me
it was me
it was always me
and never you.

What to wish for

My mother gave me arthritis when I was born
it was the least harmful disease she could

think of

in labour.

Like blood memory.

Some mother's thought their thoughts of this

or that, the most begin ailment a woman could think of
while in childbirth would be the

one that most afflicted the child throughout life.

Some of the mother's only thought happy thoughts
forgetting about what they were

supposed to think of

and now those children are no longer thought of

like stars fallen and not

wished on.

And one who gathers...

flowers dear

gather many flowers,

my wolf seeds are red

in meadows lower than the world

and pearls before pigs can only be washed

washed away

touch time with your tongue for me

my dear

my rivers are deep and wet,

at the bottom are the bones of

a god who

held madness in high esteem.

I hate my father's Sunday poems

I stabbed myself with a kitchen thermometer
and passed out before I could read it,
turned into the best sleep I've had

since I was a child

dreamed

in the backseat of my father's car
moon following

picnic beer on his breath
all the way home.

All the numbers covered in blood

SYSM is a shut your savage mouth system TIC

The loneliness of the two Voyager spacecraft

40 000 years is a long time to wait for you
but I guess I'll always be waiting at 18 000 mi/sec.

more or less.

I floated before I discovered gravity.

You'd think I'd be happy
I think of death so much.

Money cheapens everything.

When the government lottery tells me to dream big
I imagine seizing the means of production or
nationalizing the electricity grid of my province with
only the power of my voice.

I pay more lottery taxes, dream big and wonder
what Marx would have thought.
Then I go and mispronounce Marx with money.

My cat tells me that the reason cats sleep 20 hrs a day
is that, they also love songbirds?

I can't have a nap because the woman is marching on
the floor upstairs and the boy downstairs is playing
the music she's marching to.

TV should stand for not living inside. and yet its standing inside the living room?

Remember people the way they want to be remembered, the ones you hate, do not remember.

Your ego is your mountain, do not climb it, sit.
let it be the meadow it needs to be.

Charity has no value, that's what makes it meaningless.

I want to get a black dog and name him Whitey
just to see
how long it takes people to realize
the dog doesn't care.

When they pulled me out of line for "random searches"
at the airport, do not pity me for it or be angry at them,
it was for you
only you.

Laughter is the best medicine, but death doesn't care.

Pandemics making-me-manic

My mind is full of prison(s) where

I do time for various thought crime(s),

mostly,

living, or what one might interpret as living,

which,

is actually

dying

at length(s)

Antiphon with a digging sound

I know where I'm going

and I'd rather go alone,

that's what makes me different from other men.

Nietzsche once said no one *should read his work*

my

canonical hours counted in syllables

and syllabus

there meaning becomes meaningless

the spade I use

begins to

burns hot.

Maid in Hollywood
for Butterfly McQueen 1911-95

After Hollywood gave up on its racism,
McQueen left the lots,
moved to Harlem. the other H'ch,

in a white man's ear.

After her 100th role as a maid

to Katherine Hepburn, John Wayne and/or Vivian Leigh.

Prissy, Lulu, and Lottie

left Los Angeles.

We know some ceilings are

not

breakable,

even for Butterflies.

While I cut peaches and the phone rings

you live with him
you lay with him
and
you lie to yourself

you cannot come to me
in the night
rouse me from my rest
like a scratch on the door
paw into my bed

learning me line by crooked line, crows feet,
time is scarred on the skin

you cannot press down on my tongue, even
in literary terms.

a breeze under a stanza is only a blow job
under a sheet.

and tombs are for hiding dead things in.

the sound of the breathe on my lips
is not you saying any of that.

There is a dead man in my dreams and
I know who killed him

an ideal stranger
a kiss between us, these dark
broken places of me

I never recognize them

or that peaches bleed red only after the phone rings.

Finding white space

White space is always a field of battle for some

a field of power

a field for my own brown skin to lie in.

A white space is a field

that is all up hill for some, and down hill

for others, you gotta know

the *terrain* as they say

White space is stubborn and mawkish

and delicate, like iron is delicate,

white space is unrestrained and overrated.

Some say white space is finding freedom

I have not found freedom in a

space that is white, yet.

I am not done. yet.

Remember Nancy

There is rhythm in
a rope and intonation too
and they're cherubs that're
long vowels iambs

the form the foot the feet
er-e formidee babble as to be
substantial/submittable

need not rhyme
just keep tyme
vice the versa
or
verse the vice

that is
X-phrasis
oasis

to me

eyeballs and duelling drams
where metonymy and meter
die routinely

no end rime
no fooling
no way
out
no

just say
no.

Porsches not people poem

My neighbourhood disintegrates
into real estates

something only recognized as property

fee simple
legal fiction(s)

gentrification
tenements.
slumlord property management companies

intensification leads to my final destination

perhaps the rich man will come looking and find me there
rousing me from my repose

and say to me
"Dear sir, you don't suppose you may mover over a bit?"
And I might say to him
something like
"Yes my good man, take this shovel from my hand,
while I open the gate and bring your friends too."

Song in the manner of the military

Despair despair despair
is everywhere
lets all have some joy

joy joy was a baby boy,
they tore his foreskin off
and sent him off to war

and now he is no more

dis-membered his body
dis-membered his brain

now he'll never be the same

despair despair despair
is everywhere, without
any joy to be found

Sheets to die for

This sheet must never touch the
ground.

This sheet must be folded a special
way.

This sheet cannot be rolled up,
thrown into the closet, like a regular sheet.

Place your hand up in the air
whenever you see it, I mean,
over your heart.

People must be beaten,
die for this sheet.

shit, I mean shit.

This is way I am kind to strangers

I am marked

my body/ is a bruise to blue
eye
uniform

I dis/figured in your
mind
by your i/gnorance
of me

is why
I am kind to strangers

and dogs love me.

Food issues

Seen walking to work, while
the evening star still rising through
it's Hesperian moods.

mostly morning, seething into the dying of the road

two crows swash-buckle
bare, harassing a cat,
a mouse squealing
it it's maw

both crows
lunge at the cat,
cat drops mouse,
mouse escapes
under a car

My only escape
in front of one.

Plant food

August somewhither
the last American bomber left Afghanistan,
the Yankee beast *stumbered* out the
Tora Bora mountains
as sleepily as it walked in,

rubbed its swollen eyes.

Opened its opium arse, irrigated
integrated, blessed
until bloody
fertilized with hurt,
happy ending, falling vapours,
planes headed west.

Voting me off the island

The rhythm of rest
the sonic of death
the arsonist is a fortune-teller by
gunsmoke.
Strips of are missing from my life.
I am verse at verist, lamented
lambasted
hammer
anvil,
fractured in my mouth
The beauty of aboriginal man.
Options.
government designated
enemy by omission.
Prison,
trial-by-cop,
choices divide

Transference

I wish I was an iguana,
slum mocking,
tasting the angularities,
on a vine.
Sisyphean flies
are so sesquipedalian.

A cemetery in Gaza

The shells landed in the graveyard
killing, the already dead
the mourners saved from being alive
anymore.
the bodies flew up,
as the bombs hit,
the dead belonged to the air
briefly.

Empty mortar shells
became ashtrays and flower pots.

Speaking to the average Joe with inner voice

Take the extra hours, work the holidays.
Christmas is coming and the kids need teeth, *why?*
I don't know. The old lady wants to go to that new
restaurant and you haven't had a blowjob in months.
Welcome back buddy to the rest
of your-low-priced-existence.

Your boss is in FLA-dda and the prick
who holds your death-paper
is skiing somewhere nice, somewhere you'll never be.
You are at work,
dummy,

When you boss asks you to come in early, do so
don't think about it, cause you gave that up long ago
not thinking was icing on the cake,
a cake you didn't get to eat
because you had to work,
dummy.

And that raise you didn't get, they ate that too, opened
it up like it was a big giant clam and swallowed it whole
and then they fucked all night, but the one that got
fucked hardest was you,
only you weren't there, you weren't invited.
You had to work,
dummy.

This is your existence, you can't call it a life,
you gave that up.
Who knows when you did?
And that space where it used to be,
you fill it with meaningless things,
and why do you do that?
because you are dumb
and because you don't remember, you
don't know you are, you don't think,
you were never trained for that,
You just can't think!

Things abandon in the night

What is it you want to tell me after all this time,
that your life is after midnight,
safely away from me,
that you're moving to another town in another country,
you broke
your heart again and your children
never call you
and that your lonely and that your getting married
and moving to Bermuda
to pour what's left of me in you into the ocean,
that you are done with all this destiny-dross and
fate-fakery,
that the universe misspoke when it spoke our names,
that the ocean is being emptied
and it's still beautiful and it still has waves and you cry
every time you see it, say that
was only us, like message in a bottle, lost to the waves,
lost to time, sagging above the deep, poured out,
drifting away.

Eden beside the highway

As a boy
I took

frogs, beetles and fireflies from God's garden,

the sky would not fit into my jar,

nor the savage stars.

dreamers maunder more than any,
and are travellers-treasured least.

Ask Cassandra,

If I were at your deathbed/I would tell you the name
Sandra comes from the name/ Cassandra, a beautiful
dreamer/never believed/She was/is/ and is evermore placed
in thy stars as are you/beautiful dreamer.

And then my voice was waste

and the voice of the lord

remontant,

rorulent.

Respired me, saying. What does man value?

and I did not understand value or trees or thee,
it is human tears that water the Garden of
God, I said.

Chief Wahoo/yahoo has gone missing
the *Redskins* have gone missing
All of my rebellions, I have abandoned
My manifesto's anchored
to the wind
My covenant(s) broken
like clay-tablets
in the hand of man
w. of God.

God is not threatened by the female body.
The words of God cannot be added to or lessened.
w. of God.

The peace that God will send for thee
will be deep
that all may be buried in it

and in his eternity, hope to
forget
that he ever met, anyone
named Adam.

I ain't that cat-in-the-box and nether are you

The way they say
you died, was dumb.
but it was always going to be something stupid, wasn't?
It was always going to be a rap at the door
in the middle of the night,
a who are you? and who am I?
You never really know the embrace of a porch light,
talking to a stranger,
about you.
I knew it was going to be like this,
sudden.
The man standing in front of me
uniform
tailored to intimidate
he's all head games and a 9mm strapped to his brains.
He's here to play with my head like it's a pinball machine.
He says to me
I don't hear a word
I just start remembering
you.

Stromata

For those allowed to live long enough

you may have a star beside your name,

a medal if you like,

stapled to your chest

they're only paper,

so it won't hurt.

words like ni, chi and lye
nay be used
if they be new,

they will have to be inspected
in my mouth
and later institutionalized
in my mind.

back to creation

the first time man came out, he was born
then he was vomit

now he's shit

Anthropocene age
scientists are like that,
new men?

How do you say *Men who doomed their future?*
Men who doomed...?

silence.

death will be louder in the future
death will be the future
it always was
life will be the future too
it always is

both offer nothing,

suffering
without doubt,
absolutely

those who wish for deserts will get rain
those who wish for rain will get

sweet sweet sweet sweet ~~*fuck all*~~

I hate like hell to say it, Jeremiah was right,

This is *terra firma*, it was firm,
and then it was torn up, soon we can call it

terra-nullus-all-of-us

our majic number was 2,1,0, -1, min-us and then you.

first me, *first me*, because I'm a canary.

and then the bumble bee and the great inland sea and
anything else that rimes with thine

word of God.

See I learned it when I was inside one of their jails, its
not like anyone ever wrote me letters but all they had in
the place were copies of the bible and psalm books, but
I did find a copy of Dostoevsky's *Crime & Punishment*
and the amazingly, I found the time to read it. [Work] I
began to understand why our range went on lockdown
every weekend and our toilets got plugged with sheets
and pillows. the guards called it contra ban, Fyodor
called it: *sin*.

Poems are word crimes,
I'm never convicted of/they are ganged in my fingers.
Sliced off my tongue.

sometimes a poet becomes so melody with txt/he
forgets harmony of form.

being suicidal is you have a relationship with fate
its best to have a drink   it's best not to get drunk
it's best not to argue with fate.

He considers his life more than he considers his death,
is ~~suicidal~~, logical.
I often think about drowning
I cannot swim
I'd be too busy panicking to try saving myself.
I wouldn't have to think
anymore, anything, Anthropocene. After I'm seen, obscene.

Yeah I'm the Indian that choose revolution over reservation mother~~fuckerearth~~. That once there was a river
>there was a fish
>there a duck
>there was a turtle
>There is a river

changing course

>there is a duck
>there is a turtle

My nakedness came to me in a year: ekphrasis/ecphrasis/elegant gnat extraordinarily empty.

The graves in Kamloops keeps haunting me;

In this part of the garden the birds don't sing
in this part of the garden the frogs don't sing
in this part of the garden all that's heard is
the ping
of spade on bone.

Dammed the poets! even when you want to have a rebellion, they're against it against-me *Aghast.*

We are resistances/re-sentences

I don't know how to live anymore;

they climbed into my brain and took all Indian land away because the Indian(s) did not improve it: Lockean interlocutor, *and my landlord continues to own this grotto of nobody cared.*

Aristotle said it would be this way,
some would be *snared*, by mistake as it were,

a slip of the pen of fate:

You cannot return it.

a suffering is always mistaken for a misery.

I heard the prophetess at a tent revival/my mother
went to one of their residential
schools and they took out her tongue/*everybody speaks
to God in tongues, but us.*
where I lived as a child, we were visited by a library
bookmobile, I found a universe - a new darkness.

I learned reading was a way to be herd(un) heard

to see and not see and knot see and not/e/see.

if one man spend his days reading,

murdering in a book,

the one writing it would be Cain.

We are synapses in the mind of god.
Half the world sings to God with a Kalashnikov
how will he ever hear my pen, over
the other half, with cannons?

PEACE TO YOU/PEACE UPON YOU/PEACE GO WITH YOU

PEACE TO YOU/PEACE UPON YOU/PEACE GO WITH YOU

PEACE TO YOU/PEACE UPON YOU/PEACE GO WITH YOU

PEACE TO YOU/PEACE UPON YOU/PEACE GO WITH YOU

PEACE TO YOU/PEACE UPON YOU/PEACE GO WITH YOU

PEACE TO YOU/PEACE UPON YOU/PEACE GO WITH YOU

PEACE TO YOU/PEACE UPON YOU/PEACE GO WITH YOU

PEACE TO YOU/PEACE UPON YOU/PEACE GO WITH YOU

These are the most powerful words in any language.

GOD words.

YOU say them yourself.

say them EVERYTHING

god says them.

II

I am a beast in flowers/poems on petals/then dry
bones on my lips/even
they become dirt. The frogs, dead in my pocket.

dead; free from food/free from fear/free from forever.

I am a beast to a strawberry
and writers spend most of their time wrestling cats off
keyboards.

The graves in Kamloops keep haunting me;

Lenore Lenore buried under the school house floor
who went to residential school and is no more
quoth our Raven.

America who put the mundane in murder
and made raping humanity, a banality

I stand, I will take my breathe and exhale
a new reality to make my vespers
life is about nothing
life is about nothing
life is about nothing

and once you learn that
you can live it.

Come into my words

The philosopher's river never remembers me

I am anew man
a new man
a-new-man
amen
I am
amen.

III

w. of God
The One, years cannot cling to.

God has come against thee
and He will not build the new
Jerusalem here.
Mortar cannot be made of blood
to build a house of God.

The poor are the whore of the world,
the rich man's mistress,
saith the gospel of Marx.

and

The ~~warts~~ on terror are paradoxes.
saith the angel Galbraith

In the end I will not last
in the end the mirror always lies.

And our lives, will always go unfinished
and unrecognized,

but to the dead of the Golden Gate bridge,
all death ends in peace.
w. of God.

gunshot
In death, it's only you
and truth, it's either that
or it's nothing.

I have an idea for a poem, it's called *Hello Calvin,
goodbye Marien-Klage!* I want to write well ~~andwhile~~
watching my mind fall apart, Einstein was
outnumbered, everyday.

*They did not understand using force against me did not
make me ~~un~~forceful, it made me formidable.*

Years lived, clinging to the
my skin,
rusted ravens of iron,

verdigris,

beat from the heat
wrecked by sweat
bleeding gods,
Praise be to God
I am human,
To the one the years, cannot cling to,
He will be called
lord of the rising
the one, the years cannot touch
or know.

IV

I want all the days you died inside
and the whys
I want all the times you've given in or given up
given to me or given up for died.
w. of God.

When I was a child I kissed the waves of the waking,
pray to the god of my high art to bless my liver
and not my heart.
the moon tide holding me like a spell.
looking for something or someone to give my life to,
the only one who wanted it was death.

Now the entire earth will become Pompeii.

and then I wrote,
at least Ganymede served Gods   while

Persephone left her lover's iron-heart prison
inhaling spring's spurs

It was like that for us,
the rain
the hell
the goodbye, the blink of an eye
and our lives went ~~un~~changed forever

"ONE DAY GRAVITY WILL DISAPPEAR AND
THEN YOU WILL FALL IN LOVE WITH ME!"

Persephone: "UP YOURS."

why mosquitoes live in amber, some of us are like that.

I am aboriginal man
uncivilized, unrecognized
gifted to god only, and left to live outside the law(s)
of ~~White~~man,
murdered in the eyes of God, near Gaza, we are
Adam also
but only in death

I am Adam also, but
only in death.

To die like dog(s).
and they say I am cynical.

Thus spike Tonto.

And

To Rome: his hollow guise
he wears in these days,
theses-winters-of-his-times

All who live in Rome, die in Rome

God will not come down from
his holy mountains to visit thee.

Blessed are they that hustle-on-earth
for they shall not be hassled-in-heaven

Blessed are they that work-the-graveyard
for they shall rest-in-peace

most blessed, nothing

being nothing.

Anyone who dies, must go for help
Anyone who dies, must leave us, the living
hope, knowledge, and love
mostly love
mostly knowledge
mostly hope
Amen.

These days will not be remembered as plain and simple,
but from here on as,
flash and pan.
Blessed are they that work for peanuts for they
shall know the circus that is life.
w. of God.
Thy voice is diaphanous and delicate

as waves of cool water flailing my skin
GOD WILL NOT RELEASE ME FROM HIS
MOUNTIAN, NEITHER WILL HE SEND ME AWAY.

What God gives is light
What I offer back to God, is light

My daylight festers the darkness
in this, God delights.
precision is beauty, because it comes from God.

The young are condemned to the future,
the old,
to memory.

Anything called Neo is not new.
Everything is only once.
thus said someone somewhither.

If I could get near the sea
I would write my manifesto
on the tentacles of jellyfish.
thus,

When I met my life I did not recognize it
It's suffering, I wore like a cloak against the world
starved that it might eat
puked that it might be cleansed
and then it died
making me holy and sad
at the same time.

some things are synchronous, just not this.

V

Prayers are sand in the hand to man, when to God

He will not hear you,
there is so/too much
much blood on them

Any.
w. of God

Climate Change
*The Four Horsemen of the apocalypse will come
and it will be confused.*

Do not grieve him. He
does not answer. He
does as He pleases.
He, whose days know no number.
Whose beauty is the spark in man
and of all life.
[Interlocutor]

Death
is that nocturnal thunder,
the living refuse to hear.
w. of God

Blessed are the plumbers because our lives are shit
Life is a circle, but our toilets will not flush.
w. of Man.
Do not grieve him. He
does not answer. He
does as He pleases.
He, whose days know no number.
Whose beauty is the spark in man
and of all life.
[Interlocutor]

How can there be meaning in what men do?

When God's mouth is a wound
and a womb at the same time
it is winter, in my mind and I hear it cracking from memory
and on to memory.

We are all Prometheus,

    it is the spark that,
God bends time over man's back

for the theft.

Even gold and silver become like sand in the hand of man,

Bankers and murders present their services
to the ninth hell.

thus saith Dante.

Revolutions prove that the world is never ready for change.

w. of God

My hands, adjusted
clasping vespers
falling off my maw
hair like a calyx against the cold,
cantabile in its mystery and misery.

The word loud and clear

in my ear.

Attempted suicide is an attempt to escape,

better the poor lose their lives
instead of their jobs.

Thy words are rib-sticking,
like gravy.

w. of God.

Man no longer knows God
or has need of him

The w. of god is lovely and aloof,

daphnean, with doves all around

w. of God
is terrifying/edifying

shaping the sound of mega-death
to men, made of mud, (living in mud)
do not neglect the chaos coming.

There is a beauty to you I can never know in this life.

If a woman says to herself her unborn child should
not enter the world than what God could argue
with a mother's grief, and the world no longer fit for
human beings?

Love her.

w. of God.

It was the year Hades became spring and she told me
she missed Johnny Mathis.

I sit alone at night and wonder how reality is/it that
non-words are code

for how we feel?

I have given up on understanding, why mosquitoes
chose to live in amber.
chaos is never permanent.

God can raise the dead, but not the brain-dead.

And there must be structure in attacking the structure

And the universes' is God thinking.

The future is always in front of you,
look into it do not stare.

Dreams can only recognize you
while you are sleeping.
One cannot grab a sword or a pen without hope.

It is easier to live life without faith, than without food,
thus saith Sartre
[I have always followed
the sirens to my own doom

counting the lives, I've lived

in the number of times I've died
knowing,

there is nothing worth more

than

beauty

some rocks

and some waves

smashing].

Look! *Look!* he comes

writhe and weakened with word

If I never have children I would teach them to dance
to whales musings

all the notes, wet.
These days most people die of loneliness.
instead if something nice, like

lions' mouths.

how weak they must be in their faith
to have to go to temple weakly
some of them bi-weakly.

The devil making you do something is more of a
literal matter
than a matter of freewill.

This is the end of eons and aeons,

the idea of a false god is only an idea, a God could
have.

Life is sad, this is why mothers cry.

Few people are like lilacs, many are like lice.

w. of God

O.

They have emptied the schools
now all that is left is shame

if I had drowned when I was three it would have
been a life well-unlived,
even if I'd been accorded the privilege of exile I have
no place to go,

I gave to the poor, now they suffer like God.
God is my boundary and my bounty
graceful-cheerful-spirit who
colonized man or the soul of man.
[Interlocutor] of thunder.

Like a ravine or a rush of water his voice is to me
everlasting to everlasting, everlasting-lasting

amen to amen to amen to amen.
Geese pass in the night as does the life of man
nothing changes but the seasons.
God is forgetful-many

are wanting.

Religion is a creation of the other.
w. of God.

somewhither time is an echo
and death, is the sleep sacred to God

is sound and all meteors are broken before they
shine.

deconstruction is denunciation of txt
and the Lord's metric is his own
jellied in its ether and
its own word.

The most hideous crimes against humans
always take place in the broadest of daylights.

My existence was debated is 1550
in Valladolid Spain
by two monks
and once proved, I no longer existed.

I was no longer a creation of God
but the property of Man.

I am invisible
and not invited
to live

I am
divisible
I am
Indian

and in the way

all the reserve houses are made out of paper
because they are made by WASPS.

Even a stranger is closer to me than I am
[Interlocutor]

When the wealthy see the poor
they thank God and blame the poor
And no man shall be detained in death
w. of God

The work of man fades like a sound
all creation fades away like a sound
all a dust
all faded

The grass grows, the river flows and the planet burns.
There are not enough milk cartons for all the species
missing from earth.
~~drink milk~~

A child will flutter like an eel
in air
in water, in the hand of its mother

a child will flutter like
a butterfly from the hand of its mother
chasing autumn
mother stay

Some people believe being good brings them prizes,
it does
not.

In death/debt there are no prizes.

www.ingramcontent.com/pod-product-compliance
Lightning Source LLC
Chambersburg PA
CBHW061751070526
44585CB00025B/2857